G

Nerj e

MÁL GA

Authors

Cristina Liñán Baena

Yolanda del Rosal Padial

Luis-Efrén Fernández Rodríguez

Instituto de Investigación Cueva de Nerja

Fundación Pública de Servicios Cueva de Nerja

"The past of the Earth is no less important than that of Man. [...] Just as an ancient tree retains the record of its life and growth, the Earth retains memories of the past inscribed both in its depths and on its surface, in the rocks and in the landscape."

Declaration of the Rights of the Memory of the Earth, **Digne-les-Bains, France, 1991**

Hall of the Cataclysm, formation known as "The Cannon"

Plan of Nerja Cave, Show Galleries

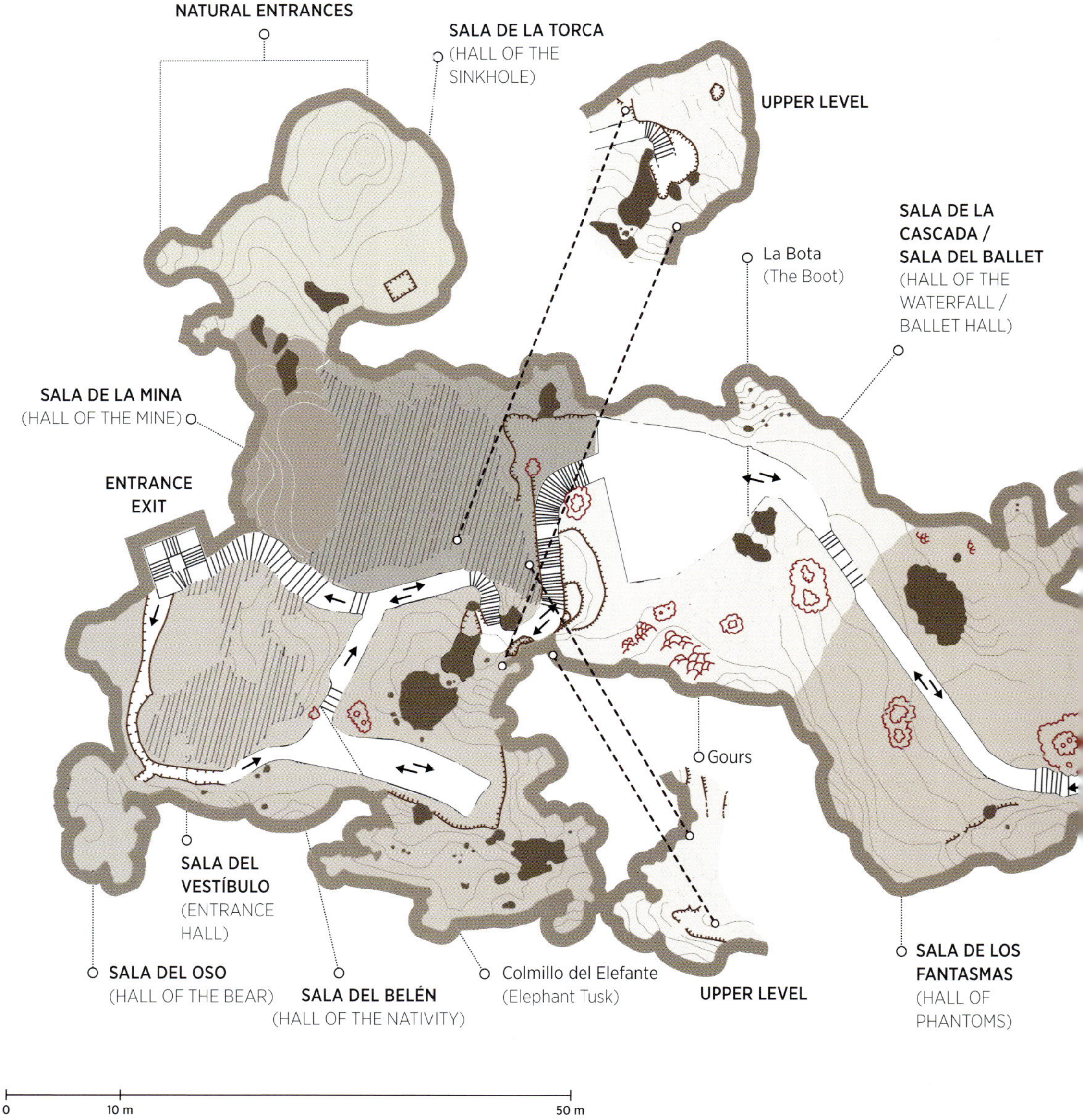

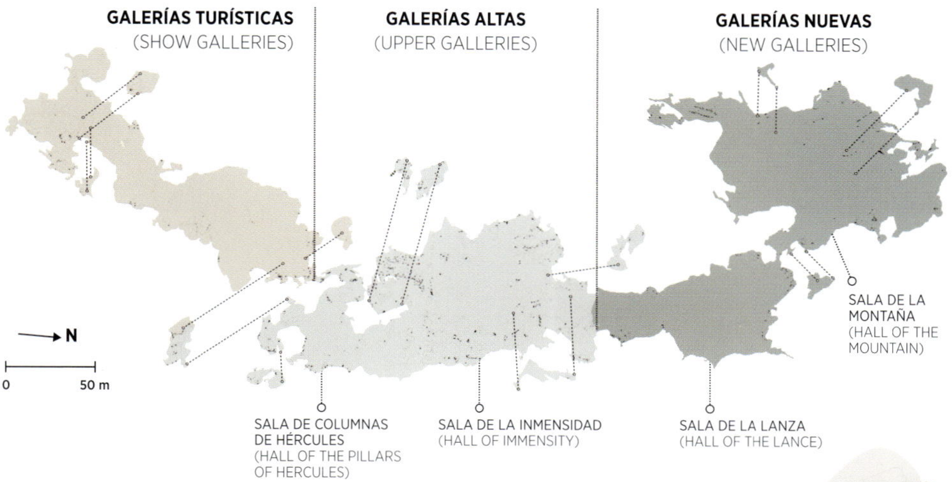
GALERÍAS TURÍSTICAS
(SHOW GALLERIES)
GALERÍAS ALTAS
(UPPER GALLERIES)
GALERÍAS NUEVAS
(NEW GALLERIES)
SALA DE LA MONTAÑA (HALL OF THE MOUNTAIN)
N
0
50 m
SALA DE COLUMNAS DE HÉRCULES (HALL OF THE PILLARS OF HERCULES)
SALA DE LA INMENSIDAD (HALL OF IMMENSITY)
SALA DE LA LANZA (HALL OF THE LANCE)

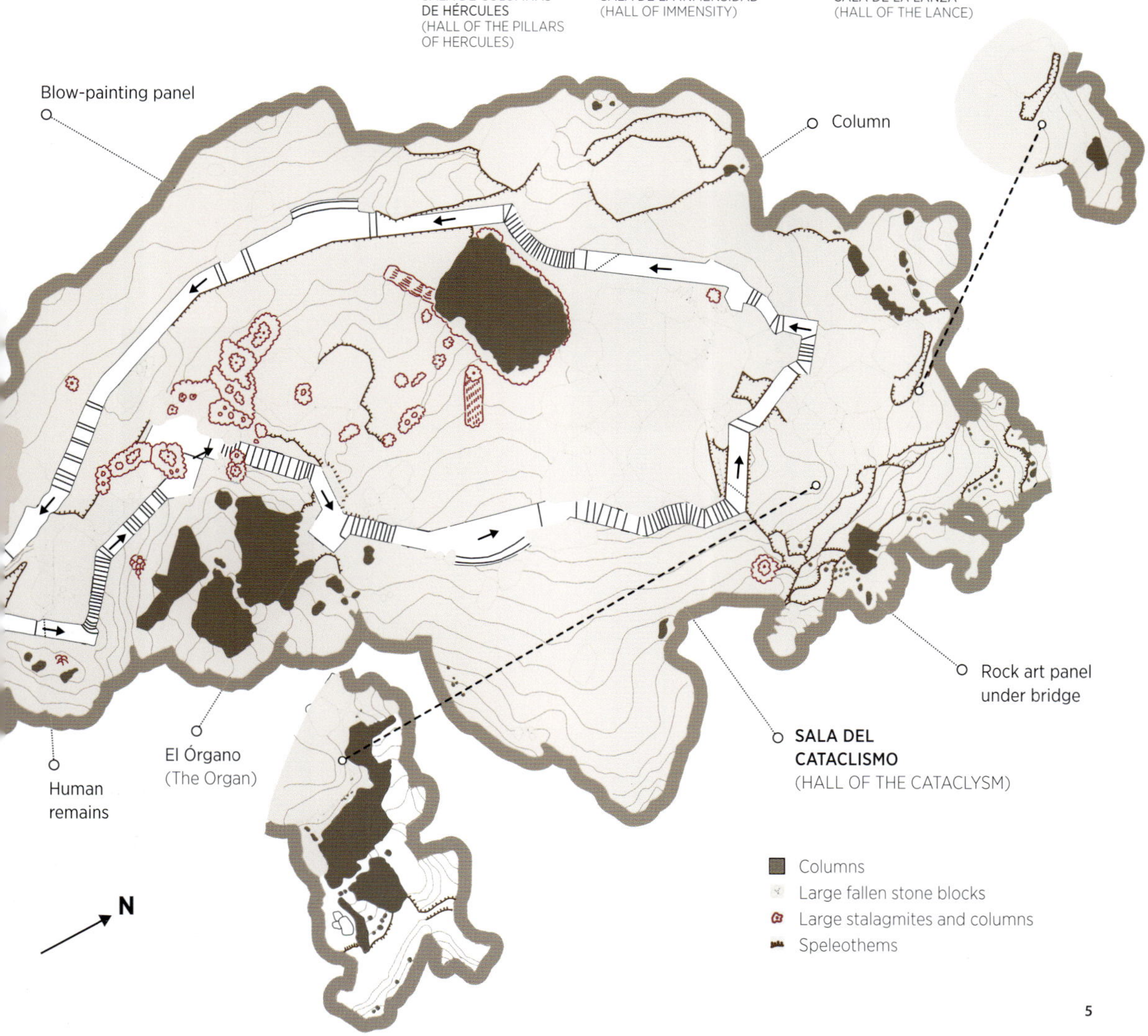
Blow-painting panel
Column
Rock art panel under bridge
SALA DEL CATACLISMO
(HALL OF THE CATACLYSM)
El Órgano
(The Organ)
Human remains
N
Columns
Large fallen stone blocks
Large stalagmites and columns
Speleothems

Timeline

Geological epochs

MIOCENE

PLIOCENE

5.33 MA

2.59 MA

Prehistoric ages

LOW

2.85 MA

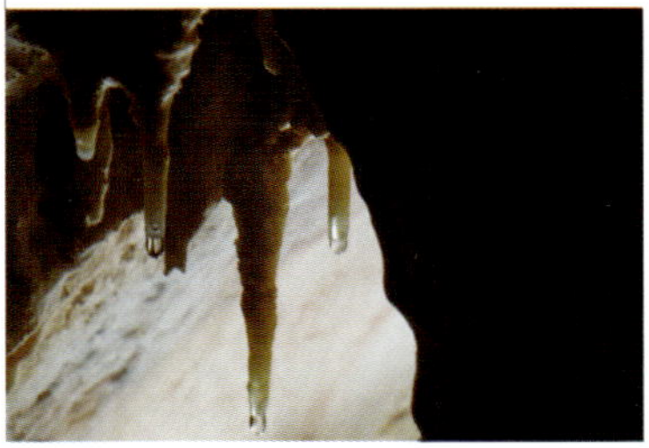

5.00 MA
Formation
of Nerja Cave

2.00 MA
Tectonic uplift elevates the
mountains, raising the
cave above the water table

External fauna occupy
the cave

800,000 BP
Major earthquake

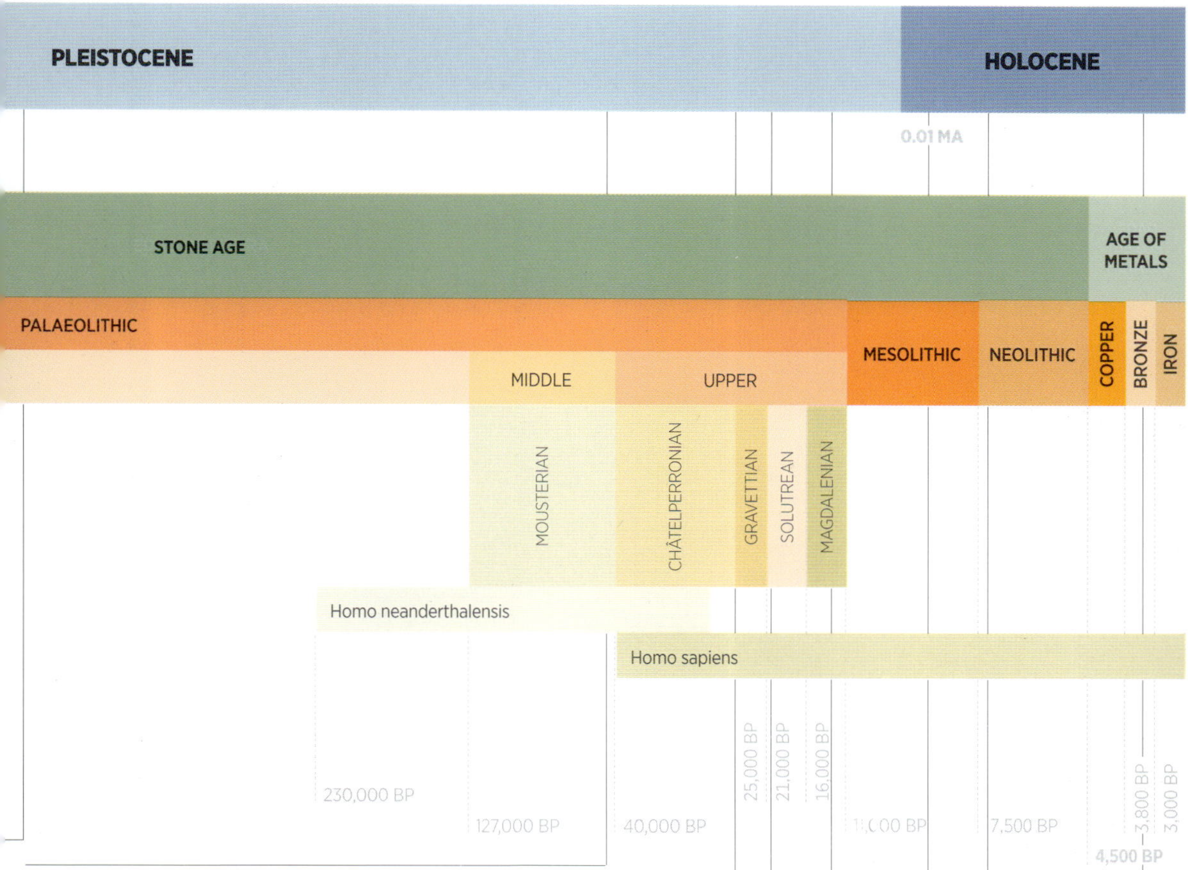

50,000 BP
First record of human presence in the cave

25,000 BP
Gravettian. Human occupation alternates with the presence of hyenas in the caverns

3,500 BP
Copper Age. Burials. Cave entrance is sealed

20,000 BP
Solutrean. First artistic expressions

12,000 BP
Magdalenian. Seal hunting

9,000 BP
Epipalaeolithic. Shell-fishing

7,000 BP
Neolithic. First farmers

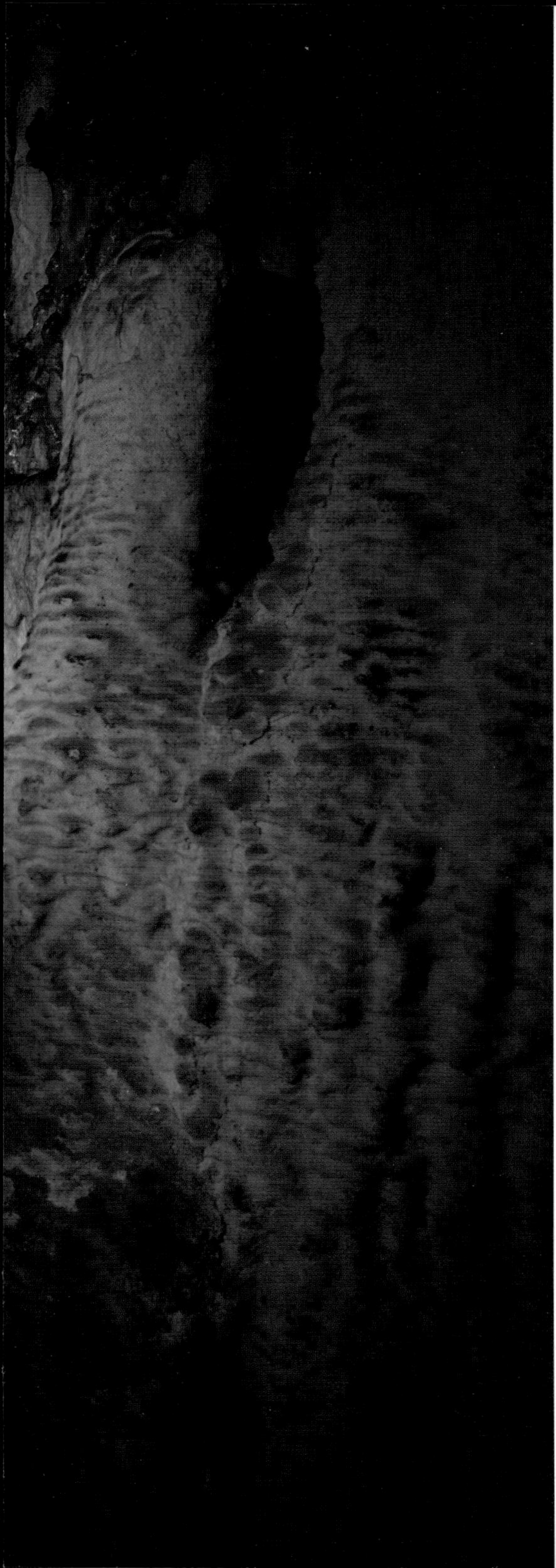

TABLE OF CONTENTS

Choosing the right place was essential to prehistoric artists

A Tour of Nerja Cave

Stalagmite in the Hall of Phantoms

NERJA CAVE, AN ACCESSIBLE PARADISE

Nerja Cave is located at the eastern end of the province of Málaga in the Axarquía region, about four kilometres outside the town of Nerja and very close to the picturesque village of Maro. It stands in a spot of singular beauty, nestled between the blue sea and rugged coastline of the Maro-Cerro Gordo Cliffs and the peaks of the Sierras Tejeda-Almijara-Alhama Natural Park. This part of the Costa del Sol boasts an unparalleled climate, with very mild temperatures year-round.

The cave has a surface area of 35,000 m^2 and a volume of approximately 300,000 m^3, making it one of the largest cavern systems in Andalusia. Evocative names like the Hall of Immensity or Hall of the Mountain illustrate the colossal size of some of the underground chambers. The route through the cave, riddled with labyrinthine twists and turns, is nearly five kilometres long, although the linear distance from one end to the other is only about 700 metres. The halls and galleries are roughly aligned along a north-south axis, with a maximum elevation difference of 68 metres.

The cave has three natural entrances and is divided into three sections: the Show Galleries, the Upper Galleries and the New Galleries. Only the first are open to visitors. As the average temperature inside the cave is 19º C, warm clothing is not necessary. However, it is advisable to wear closed-toed shoes with non-slip soles as there are more than 400 steps along the tour itinerary.

View of the Sierra Almijara and the Nerja coast

Entrance Hall

In prehistoric times, the Entrance Hall was completely open to the outside

Singular rock art motifs in the Niche of Fish Forms, possibly representing seals

Hall of the Mine. This space, together with the Entrance Hall and Hall of the Sinkhole, was once part of a large natural rock shelter, heavily frequented by prehistoric human groups

Listed as a Cultural Heritage Asset in the Archaeological Zone category, Nerja Cave contains one of the most important archaeological sites on the Iberian Peninsula. It is also home to an exceptional natural heritage, with vast halls and spectacular formations of great scientific interest, as well as a unique ecosystem with endemic species. To ensure the cave's conservation, a protective buffer zone of nearly three million square metres has been established on the surface.

THE SHOW GALLERIES

The tour of Nerja Cave begins at a staircase built in 1959, taking advantage of an ancient sinkhole that had filled up with dirt and rocks, known to Maro residents as *Hoyo del Espino* or Hawthorn Hole. This staircase leads to the first space, the Entrance Hall, thus named because it is one of the three chambers—the other two being the Hall of the Mine and Hall of the Sinkhole—from which the cave can be accessed.

These are the rooms once inhabited by prehistoric humans, which would have had natural light in ancient times. The cave mouths were filled in gradually by natural processes after the last human occupations at the end of the Copper Age, between 4,500 and 3,800 BP approximately.

Hall of the Nativity

A narrow passage carved out of the rock leads from the Entrance Hall to the intermediate area of the cave system, the Hall of the Nativity and the Hall of the Elephant Tusk. The Hall of the Nativity owes its name to the fact that some of the natural formations resemble traditional Christmas nativity scenes. After touring this chamber, we pass through the Hall of the Elephant Tusk and enter the innermost section of the Show Galleries.

The cave has a surface area of 35,000 m² and a volume of approximately 300,000 m³, making it one of the largest caverns in Andalusia.

Hall of the Waterfall / Ballet Hall

Convenient steps overcome the considerable drop down to the Hall of the Waterfall, the first area of

Hall of the Sinkhole, with the archaeological dig in the foreground and the sinkhole in the ceiling

Upper galleries of the Hall of the Nativity

Entrance to the Hall of Phantoms

Hall of the Nativity

Stalagmites that gave the Hall of Phantoms its name

the cave discovered by explorers. It is named after a group of tiered formations resembling a stone waterfall, called gours or rimstone dams. This room is also known as the Ballet Hall because, given its spaciousness and remarkable beauty, it has hosted the International Music and Dance Festival since July 1960. Legendary names like Mstislav Rostropovich, Maya Plisetskaya, Joaquín Cortés, Alfredo Kraus, Montserrat Caballé, José Carreras and Paco de Lucía have performed here.

This vast chamber contains an impressive column known as "The Boot" and formations with evocative names like "The Capitol", "The Tower of Pisa" or "The Shield" on its upper levels.

Listed as a Cultural Heritage Asset in the Archaeological Zone category, Nerja Cave contains one of the most important archaeological sites on the Iberian Peninsula.

Panoramic view of the Hall of the Cataclysm

Hall of Phantoms

Following in the footsteps of the cave's young discoverers, we come to the Hall of Phantoms, named after a group of stalagmites whose spectral shapes cast ghostly shadows on the cave wall. However, what truly gave the youthful pioneers a fright were the human skeletons they found lying on the floor of this chamber. The idea that they might have been former visitors to the cave who could not find their way out brought the boys' first adventure to a hasty conclusion, although they later returned and helped to discover new galleries. These human remains were one of the reasons why authorities immediately decided to protect the cave and commence the archaeological research that continues to this day.

Hall of the Cataclysm

A small flight of steps leads to one of the largest underground chambers in all of Spain, the Hall of the Cataclysm. A magical landscape materialises before our eyes. Here we see a gigantic column, 32 metres high and 18 metres in diameter, registered in the Guinness Book of Records as the largest in the world, and at its foot a wild, chaotic jumble of stalagmites, stone blocks and columns. This incredible sight, which gave the hall its name, is the result of a massive earthquake that hit the region approximately 800,000 years ago, which we know of thanks to information stored in the speleothems during their slow formation process.

Evidence of the cataclysm that occurred thousands of years ago and inspired the name of the final show gallery

Gours that gave the Hall of the Waterfall its name

The designated walkway circles around the hall, giving us a chance to observe the column from every angle and appreciate the myriad facets of this spectacular natural wonder. We can also glimpse the niche that holds "The Organ", an impressive sheet-like formation on the wall decorated with a remarkable example of rock art.

At a bend in the path leading to the exit, we can see the entrance to the Upper and New Galleries. On the way back, we will also observe many rock formations of stunning beauty, including a large rock with a Pinocchio-like profile. The rear end of this hall is also the lowest point in the entire cave system, 31 metres below the current entrance.

From here we retrace our steps to the exit with the satisfaction of having seen a genuine natural spectacle, minimally modified by prehistoric humans and only slightly altered in modern times so that everyone can enjoy this subterranean wonderland.

FIVE EXPLORERS, ONE COLOSSAL DISCOVERY

The modern history of Nerja Cave began with five intrepid boys: José Luis Barbero de Miguel, the brothers Manuel and Miguel Muñoz Zorrilla, Francisco Navas Montesinos and José Torres Cárdenas. Like everyone else in Maro, their home village, the youths were familiar with a small cave they called the "cemetery mine", reached by means of two natural shafts near the old cemetery of Maro. On 12 January 1959, the five boys were inside that little cavern when they saw a large colony of bats emerge from a narrow crevice in the wall. Intrigued, they decided to do a bit of exploring ... The crevice led to a very narrow passageway, which they scrambled through with some difficulty and found themselves in a large, hitherto unknown chamber, now called the Hall of the Waterfall or Ballet Hall. As the light from their single electric torch swept across the vast geological marvel before their eyes and hundreds of bats fluttered about the cave, they were overcome by a mixture of fear and awe. They soon worked up the courage to explore new corners of the cave, and gradually began to comprehend the importance of their find. Sinking into the bat guano accumulated on the cave floor over thousands of years, they managed to make their way to the Hall of Phantoms, where they stumbled upon two human skeletons. This discovery frightened them so badly that they decided to end their adventure and beat a swift retreat to the exit.

Days later they returned to the cave, this time accompanied by two of their teachers, Manuela Mora Plaza and Carlos Saura Garre, who attested to the veracity of their discovery. Three months later, on 19 April 1959, a new expedition was organised that included a young photographer from Nerja, José Padial Bobadilla. His photos, published days later in the Málaga daily *SUR*, revealed Nerja Cave to the world and caught the attention of the authorities, the scientific community and other national media. But the story of this discovery was just beginning ...

In November 1959, one of those five boys, Francisco Navas Montesinos, eager to make new finds, resumed his exploration of the cave. This time it was not bats but air draughts that led him to a new section of the cavern, which had never been explored before as it was very difficult to access. He had stumbled upon the first halls of the Upper Galleries ... Ten years later, in 1969, the Speleology Section of the Provincial Archaeological Museum of Málaga began the first systematic speleological exploration of the cave. This work culminated in the discovery of the New Galleries, the innermost section of Nerja Cave. Today we know that the network of underground tunnels and chambers is even larger, although some spaces are so tight that speleologists have not yet been able to explore them. ❖

Natural Subterranean Wonder

Evidence of a major earthquake in the Hall of the Cataclysm, dated to 800,000 BP

HOW WAS NERJA CAVE FORMED?

Listed as a Geological Site of International Interest, Nerja Cave boasts an underground landscape of astonishing, unforgettable beauty. The best-known geological formations in this landscape are stalactites, stalagmites and columns, but they are not the only ones ... In fact, the cave is considered a veritable "speleothem museum" given the abundance, variety and splendour of the formations it contains. Speleothems (from the Greek *spelaion* = cave and *thema* = deposit) are mineral deposits that form inside caves.

The cave was formed in the dolomitic marble of the Sierra Almijara, rocks that originated approximately 240 million years ago and consist largely of dolomite, a mineral composed of calcium carbonate and magnesium. The cavern was formed by a process known as karstification: rainwater dissolves carbon dioxide from the atmosphere and especially from the ground, creating carbonic acid. The water that filters down thus becomes an "acidic", "aggressive" substance which dissolves cracks and fissures in the rock as it passes through them. This gradual dissolution creates different types of channels and hollows in the rock that grow larger over time and eventually join together to form a large cavity.

It is estimated that rainwater began to infiltrate and flow through the cracks and fissures in the marble of the Sierra Almijara over 5 million years ago, during the **Miocene**.

Throughout the **Pliocene**, the progressive dissolution of the marble produced different types of hollows and channels which merged and created a large cavity. The first speleothems began to form in the cave at the end of this epoch.

Tectonic uplift in the **Lower Pleistocene** raised the mountains of the Sierra Almijara, which in turn caused the groundwater level to drop. The cave, once partly flooded, was now above the water table. Speleothems continued to form.

The **Middle Pleistocene** was marked by various collapses in the cave, with seismic movements causing stone blocks and speleothems to fall. However, speleothems continued to grow throughout this period.

Finally, from the **Middle Pleistocene to the Holocene**, speleothem formation and growth advanced significantly, especially in warm, humid periods. The outermost chambers filled up with sand and clay from eroding adjacent slopes, carried into the cave by water flows whose volume varied depending on whether the climate was wet or dry at the time.

Water also plays a role in the formation of speleothems. After it seeps through the soil and rock, rainwater "loaded" with minerals reaches the cave, where it evaporates and/or loses its carbon dioxide content. The degasification of this water upon reaching the cave is something similar to opening a shaken bottle of soda. But at that moment the process is inverted: instead of continuing to dissolve rock, the water becomes oversaturated with minerals, and the minerals dissolved in that water are precipitated on the ceiling, floor or walls of the cavern, producing different types of speleothems. The shape of a speleothem depends on various factors, such as whether the water drips, flows, splashes, condenses or moves along the rock walls by capillary action.

Formation process of Nerja Cave

Water table
Water table
Water table
Water table
Water table

A SPELEOTHEM MUSEUM

The scientific names for many cave speleothems are quite curious, as they often refer to the shape of the deposit or the thing it most resembles. Soda straws, bottlebrushes, shields, draperies, cave pearls, cave clouds, cave cones, calcite rafts, cave rings, conulites and moonmilk are just some of the types, subtypes and varieties of speleothems found in Nerja Cave.

STALACTITE

A conical, icicle-shaped speleothem that hangs from the ceilings of caves. All stalactites start out as soda straws. When the tip of an active stalactite is submerged in a pool of water, mineral precipitation continues and forms bottlebrushes.

Large stalactites, Hall of the Cataclysm

Bottlebrushes, Hall of the Mountain

SODA STRAWS

Hollow tubular stalactites that vary in length and generally have a diameter of 1 cm at the bottom. The thickness of the tube wall ranges from 0.1 to 0.5 mm.

< Soda straw, Hall of the Nativity

STALAGMITE

A cave floor formation created by mineral-rich water dripping down from the ceiling or from a stalactite. Stalagmites usually have rounded tips. The shape and size of a stalagmite depends on many factors: distance from the drip point, drip rate, amount of dissolved mineral in the water, etc.

< Stalagmite in the Hall of Phantoms

COLUMN

A speleothem that is formed when a stalagmite and a stalactite meet. Several large columns can be seen along the show route in Nerja Cave.

Column, Hall of the Lance >

SHIELD OR PALETTE

A disc-shaped speleothem consisting of two parallel circular or oval plates of varying diameter separated by a crack. Shields are found on cave walls, ceilings or floors. When stalactites form on the bottom of a shield, it is called a "parachute".

< Shield, Hall of the Waterfall

CONULITE

A conical speleothem that forms on cave floors covered with soft substances such as mud, sand, guano, moonmilk, etc. Water dripping on this unconsolidated surface creates a hollow depression or "splash cup", the walls of which are gradually lined with calcite. In Nerja Cave, only one variety has been identified so far, a deeper, thicker cylindrical form known as a "negative stalagmite". Some negative stalagmites in the cave were used as stationary lamps by prehistoric human groups.

< Negative stalagmite used as a stationary lamp in the Upper Palaeolithic, Hall of the Cataclysm

FLOWSTONE

A speleothem made of different layers or sheets that initially follow the shape of the underlying surface or rock. When flowstone forms atop soft sediment that is later eroded, the sheet seems to "float" above the cave floor and is called a "false floor". Balloon-shaped flowstones formed on the walls and floors of underground pools or lakes are called "cave clouds".

Flowstone in the Hall of the Waterfall >

Cave clouds, Hall of the Cataclysm >

DRAPERIES

Wavy speleothems hanging from slanted ceilings or walls in a cave. They are also called curtains, angel's wings, ribbons, shawls or, in the case of draperies with coloured streaks, cave bacon.

Draperies, Hall of the Mountain

GOURS

Gours or rimstone dams are speleothems formed by water flowing down a slope in a thin sheet or on the edge of shallow pools. Small specimens are known as micro-gours.

< Micro-gours and soda straws, Hall of the Sinkhole

CAVE RING

A ring-shaped speleothem whose varying diameter is determined by the splash radius of the drip source.

< Cave ring in the Hall of the Cataclysm

CORALLOIDS

Nodular or globular speleothems, also known as cave popcorn, grapes or cauliflowers. The most spectacular coralloids in Nerja Cave are called "fingernails", and the finest examples are found in the Hall of the Mountain (New Galleries). This is a directional coralloid that develops in the splash area of water dripping from a point high enough to permit nebulisation (the formation of tiny water droplets suspended in the atmosphere). Coralloids tend to grow in the direction where there is the highest concentration of water droplets.

Coralloids, Hall of Phantoms >

"Fingernails", Hall of the Mountain >

HELICTITE OR ECCENTRIC

A speleothem that grows in any direction, defying the law of gravity. It usually forms on ceilings, walls or other speleothems and, in rare cases, on cave floors. It has a very narrow central channel (0.008–0.5 mm) through which water travels by capillary action.

Eccentrics, Hall of the Lance

CALCITE RAFT

A thin, flat speleothem of crystalline material that floats on the surface of cave pools or gours. It is usually about one millimetre thick, like a sheet of paper. Also known as floe calcite.

< Calcite raft, Hall of the Bear

CAVE CONES

The process by which these speleothems are formed is quite curious. When water drips onto a calcite raft, the impact causes it to sink. The calcite accumulates in a certain spot at the bottom of the lake, forming a cone or volcano shape whose tip is perfectly aligned with the drip source. When the lake dries up, the cones, once submerged, are exposed on the cave floor, just like the ones in the upper section of the Hall of the Nativity.

< Small cave cones, Hall of the Bear. When the sheet of water disappears, the calcite raft is deposited on the bottom and covers the floor like snowflakes.

CAVE PEARLS

Speleothems of various shapes (spherical, cylindrical, irregular, cubic and even hexagonal) with concentric onion-like layers that form in small pools of water. The different growth layers are built up around a nucleus of foreign matter, such as a small speleothem fragment, bat bone or piece of coal.

Cave pearls in the Hall of the Sinkhole

MOONMILK

A white or cream-coloured speleothem formed of aggregates of very fine crystals of varying composition. It is gooey and pasty when wet, rather like cream cheese, but crumbly when dry, resembling talcum powder. In antiquity, this speleothem was used as a cosmetic, a cure for eye ailments and a lactation stimulant for nursing mothers.

< Moonmilk, Hall of the Cataclysm

SHELFSTONE

A flat, shelf-like speleothem extending from the edge of a cave pool or attached to another speleothem (stalagmite or column) submerged in the pool. Shelfstones are indicators of past water levels in caves. When the edges are convex and extend towards the heart of the pool, it is called lily-pad shelfstone.

< Shelfstone, Hall of the Pillars of Hercules

Banding inside a speleothem. The black stripes are due to soot from prehistoric fires, alternating with layers of calcite. Hall of Phantoms

But speleothems are not just pretty decorative features ... Like other sediments deposited in the cave, speleothems are valuable scientific records of the processes that originated them and the prevalent environmental conditions (climate, hydrology, plant life, etc.) during their formation process.

For example, studying speleothems can tell us about past climate changes, as we can determine at what temperature they formed by analysing their oxygen and carbon isotopes. The average temperature inside the cave is generally the same as the average temperature outside. Therefore, the temperature at which the speleothems were formed, determined by isotope analysis, tells us what the outside climate was like at the time of their formation. Many speleothems have concentric bands which, like tree rings, contain information about the soil and plants that existed above the cave in prehistoric times.

One of the most amazing and little-known facts about speleothems is that they constitute a reliable record of the earthquakes that occurred in their region. Broken and growing stalagmites are examined to learn about palaeo-earthquakes. Scientists envision stalagmites as homogeneous cylinders attached to the ground which collapsed due to seismic waves. The diameter-to-height ratio of a broken stalagmite is an indicator of the distance from the earthquake's epicentre and its magnitude.

Another way to study palaeo-earthquakes is by analysing abrupt shifts in the growth axis or changes in the colour or texture of growth layers that are revealed in the cross-section of a stalagmite, as such changes are known to be associated with seismic events. Dating these abrupt changes makes it possible to determine the chronological sequence of earthquakes that hit a certain region in the distant past. In the case of Nerja Cave, studies show that a major earthquake occurred approximately 800,000 years before the present, the effects of which are clearly visible in the Hall of the Cataclysm.

LITTLE CAVE DWELLERS

Nerja Cave is home to a singular array of living creatures, predominantly small fauna and micro-organisms. Interactions between the different communities that inhabit this particular underground ecosystem keep it in balance and thus promote its conservation.

From a biogeographical and evolutionary perspective, some species can be classified as palaeoendemic—in other words, surviving specimens of a largely extinct population. These life forms are also of great scientific value as a source of biological substances with potential applications in medicine or other fields.

Although bats are the most familiar species, there are other animals that like the darkness of caves. Tiny creatures that have adapted to the unique conditions of these subterranean habitats make up a peculiar, vulnerable class of animals known as troglofauna or troglobionts.

Due to the absence of light and high relative humidity, troglobionts tend to have smaller eyes or no eyes at all, thin, depigmented carcasses or membranes, elongated bodies and appendages, and enhanced tactile and chemical sensory organs. The scarcity of food and the need to conserve energy have made them able to go without nourishment for an extended time; they also have a widely varied diet and lead a calm, non-aggressive existence with long periods of lethargy. Troglofauna species identified in Nerja Cave include the beetle *Platyderus speleaus* (Cobos, 1961), the cricket *Petaloptila malacitana* (Barranco, 2010), the pseudo-scorpion *Ephippiochthonius nerjaensis* (Carabajal Márquez, García Carrillo & Rodríguez Fernández, 2001), the dipluran *Plusiocampa baetica* (Sendra, 2004) and the isopod *Porcellio narixae* (Cifuentes, 2018). The last three species are all endemic to this particular cave.

With regard to microbiology, Nerja Cave is inhabited by a wide range of micro-organisms, which are usually organised in complex structured communities called biofilms. This level of organisation allows them to act in a coordinated manner and gives them greater stability and resistance to adverse external conditions. Cave biofilms tend not to be very diverse and are highly sensitive to environmental changes. Perhaps the most familiar representatives of subterranean microbiota are biofilms largely made up of phototrophic micro-organisms, commonly known as lampenflora or "green sickness". In Nerja Cave these biofilms are found on surfaces close to electric light sources and principally consist of the cyanobacteria *Chroococcidiopsis* sp. and the red algae *Cyanidium* sp., highly resistant organisms that can remain latent for years in less favourable environmental conditions. Although the activity of micro-organisms is essential to the preservation of the subterranean ecosystem, their uncontrolled growth can lead to problems such as the dissolution, corrosion, flaking or pigmentation of speleothems. This damage is particularly serious when the affected surface contains rock art, given the particular fragility of this exceptional vestige of underground cultural heritage. ❖

Rhinolophus ferrumequinum, greater horseshoe bat

Petaloptila malacitana, the most abundant troglofauna in the cave

Ephippiochthonius nerjaensis, a species endemic to Nerja Cave

Plusiocampa baetica, an example of adaptation to a subterranean environment

Porcellio narixae, a common species in the Show Galleries

Light and water facilitate the spread of "green sickness" in caves

Nerja Cave, a Landmark in European Prehistory

A beautiful corner in the Hall of the Nativity

HUMAN OCCUPATION OF THE CAVE

Archaeological excavations in Nerja Cave were begun immediately after its discovery with the initial aim, on the part of the Spanish government, of opening it to visitors as an attraction that would boost tourism on the Costa del Sol. Research has continued steadily ever since.

The human occupation of Nerja Cave began in the Palaeolithic, with evidence of their presence stretching back over 45,000 years (based on the dating of unaltered material found on the surface). This makes it one of the longest-used caves in Europe. Evidence of human activity has been found in practically every chamber of Nerja Cave; here prehistoric humans ventured further from the cave mouth than in most cases, making their way through tortuous, physically challenging passages.

The area closest to the mouth and the three outer halls (Entrance, Mine and Sinkhole) have the highest concentration of traces of daily domestic activities of prehistoric human groups. The intermediate and innermost areas—the halls of the Nativity, Elephant Tusk, Waterfall, Phantoms, Cataclysm and Upper Galleries—are where the cave's Palaeolithic inhabitants performed ritual activities with magical/religious significance. This is also true of Neolithic and Copper Age societies, in which domestic life was concentrated in sectors closest to the natural entrances, reserving the deepest parts of the cave for funerary use.

We know that the first humans to occupy the cave were either the last Neanderthal groups or the first modern sapiens. The oldest archaeological materials identified at Nerja are flint tools found on the lowest levels of the excavation in the Entrance Hall. These tools correspond to the Mousterian lithic culture and date from around 45,000 BP.

On top of these deposits, archaeologists found traces of Gravettian culture, from between 25,000 and 21,000 BP, when the cave was used alternately as a human dwelling and a hyena den and the climate was cool and relatively dry.

Later, between 21,000/20,000 and 16,000 BP, the cave was frequented by Solutrean groups, who created a large part of the "cave sanctuary" and a particularly fascinating graphic code. They inhabited Nerja Cave in a relatively wet, mild

We know that the first humans to occupy the cave were either the last Neanderthal groups or the first modern sapiens.

"The Organ" formation, Hall of the Cataclysm

climate period, when the coastline was roughly five kilometres away from the cave due to a glacial phenomenon.

These groups of hunters, fishermen and gatherers were followed by humans of the Magdalenian culture, although the only surviving evidence of their presence dates from the end of that period, around 12,000 BP, perhaps because older layers suffered the same heavy erosion observed in several areas of the outer halls. At this point, we observe changes in their lifestyle and how they interacted with both the cave and the environment. These groups are a special case of "semi-sedentary" occupation of the cave, probably

Flint point, Gravettian culture

Pecten shell used as a lamp in recent prehistory

Plaquette with a duck, Magdalenian culture

because the local climate and the abundance of natural resources allowed them to dwell in the cavern year-round. During this time, the climate alternated between cold, more or less temperate, and warm periods, as attested by faunal remains (there is even evidence of the presence of penguins). Land animals (goats, deer and rabbits) and sea creatures (monk seals and dolphins) were the basis of this population's subsistence.

At the end of the glacial period, documented in the archaeological record by the presence of marine species typical of northern seas, temperatures and sea levels rose. As a result, the sandy beaches disappeared and the coastline began to acquire its present-day configuration, dominated by impressive cliffs. This marked the beginning of the Holocene, in approximately 10,500 BP, when the cave was inhabited by Epipalaeolithic societies.

The end of the Epipalaeolithic phases, although the chronology varies from one region to the next, witnessed the progressive appearance of Neolithic societies with econ-

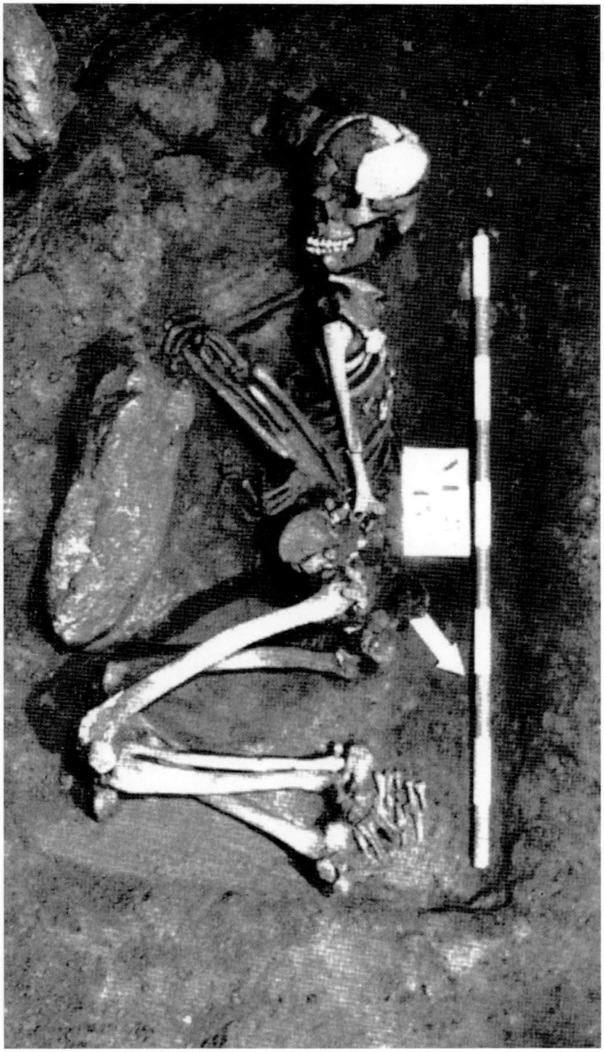

Epipalaeolithic burial of an individual dubbed "Pepita", who died around the age of 20

The human occupation of Nerja Cave began in the Palaeolithic, with evidence of their presence stretching back over 45,000 years

omies based on food production, who occupied the cave from 7,500 to 4,500 BP. In addition to the adoption of a sedentary lifestyle, fully implemented on the coast of Málaga by the late Neolithic, the development of an economy based on agriculture and animal husbandry was the defining feature of this period. There were also significant advances in everyday production utensils as the use of pottery vessels and objects, polished stone tools and flint sickle pieces became widespread.

Around 4,500 BP the Neolithic gave way to the Chalcolithic or Copper Age. Technological breakthroughs consolidated the productive economy and gradually altered the social structures of human groups, planting the seed of subsequent social stratification processes. As in the Neolithic, the entire cave was used for symbolic/funerary purposes, leaving the outermost chambers for occasional domestic use (storage, sheep pens, etc.).

LIFE AND DEATH IN NERJA CAVE

In addition to the Epipalaeolithic interment documented in 1982 in the Hall of the Sinkhole, a precursor of burial forms and rites that would be amply practised in late prehistory, when the cave was discovered in 1959 it contained abundant evidence of funerary use, from the entrances to the far end of the Hall of the Cataclysm and other remote spots deep inside the cavern. At the time of discovery, two individuals interred in an extended supine position were found in the Hall of Phantoms, which may date from the final phases of the cave's funerary use. The human remains visible at that time—burials, judging by what has come down to us and the information on record—indicate a cultural classification that places them in the late Neolithic and the Copper Age.

A tremendously important find was made when a small mound of calcareous stones, partially filling a natural niche in the Hall of the Mine, was excavated and found to contain the remains of a man and a woman in foetal position, one at each end of the tumulus. An equally significant event was the partial excavation by Professor Francisco Jordá's team of a similar mound in the Hall of the Mine, which presented reddish iron-oxide pigmentation. Recent carbon-14 dating places it in the late Neolithic, the same date assigned to similar forms found in several villages in the Vega de Antequera region of Málaga, from the early stages of megalithic culture.

The chaotic jumble of rocks at the entrance to the Hall of the Cataclysm is known as the "Pellicer corpses sector" after the first archaeologist who worked in the cave. Several skeletal remains were recovered in this area, and oral accounts of the days that followed the discovery of the cave mention the uncontrolled removal of approximately ten pottery vessels. More recently, a spherical vessel with a cylindrical neck was found in the west sector of the Hall of the Cataclysm. This object appears to be a funerary offering from the Neolithic-Chalcolithic transition period, associated with the fossilised vessel still visible in a calcareous flowstone on the south side of the same hall. ❈

Grave goods preserved in situ, Neolithic/Chalcolithic

Chalcolithic cupules, evidence of funerary rites in the cave, similar to those found on dolmen walls

Prehistoric Art

Solutrean goat, Hall of the Pillars of Hercules

Detail of rock art composition made by blow-painting

ARTISTIC EXPRESSION IN NERJA CAVE

Nerja Cave contains more prehistoric art than any other cave in Europe. Due to its great age and extreme fragility, this art is excluded from the tour itinerary and can only be seen using the audio/video guide.

Prehistoric artists primarily decorated the halls of the Nativity, Waterfall, Phantoms and Cataclysm, although there is also a spectacular pictorial composition in the Upper Galleries. In the figurative and symbolic art of Nerja Cave, there is a clear distinction between artistic expressions from the Pleistocene (Upper Palaeolithic) and those made by prehistoric societies of the Holocene—in other words, Neolithic and Chalcolithic or Copper Age humans. The latest studies conducted by Professor José Luis Sanchidrián suggest that some of the identified artworks may be even older.

Nerja Cave contains more prehistoric art than any other cave in Europe.

The greatest number of pictorial elements are found in the Solutrean "sanctuary". Divided into two groups, one archaic and another more recent, they were made between 20,000 and 16,000 years ago. Most of the figurative motifs—predominantly stags, does, goats and horses—date from this period. However, over 93% of the artwork consists of rhythmically connected linear signs and dots which, as best we can tell, constitute a graphic code used to convey ideas. Similar patterns are found in different caves throughout the province of Málaga. These signs are usually arranged around animal figures strategically situated on the chosen rock panels; the best example is "The Organ" niche in the Hall of the Cataclysm.

There is a clear predominance of red pigment, in which the main ingredient is iron oxide. Archaeological excavations

Schematic anthropomorphic figures known as "The Dancers", Hall of the Sinkhole. Neolithic/Chalcolithic

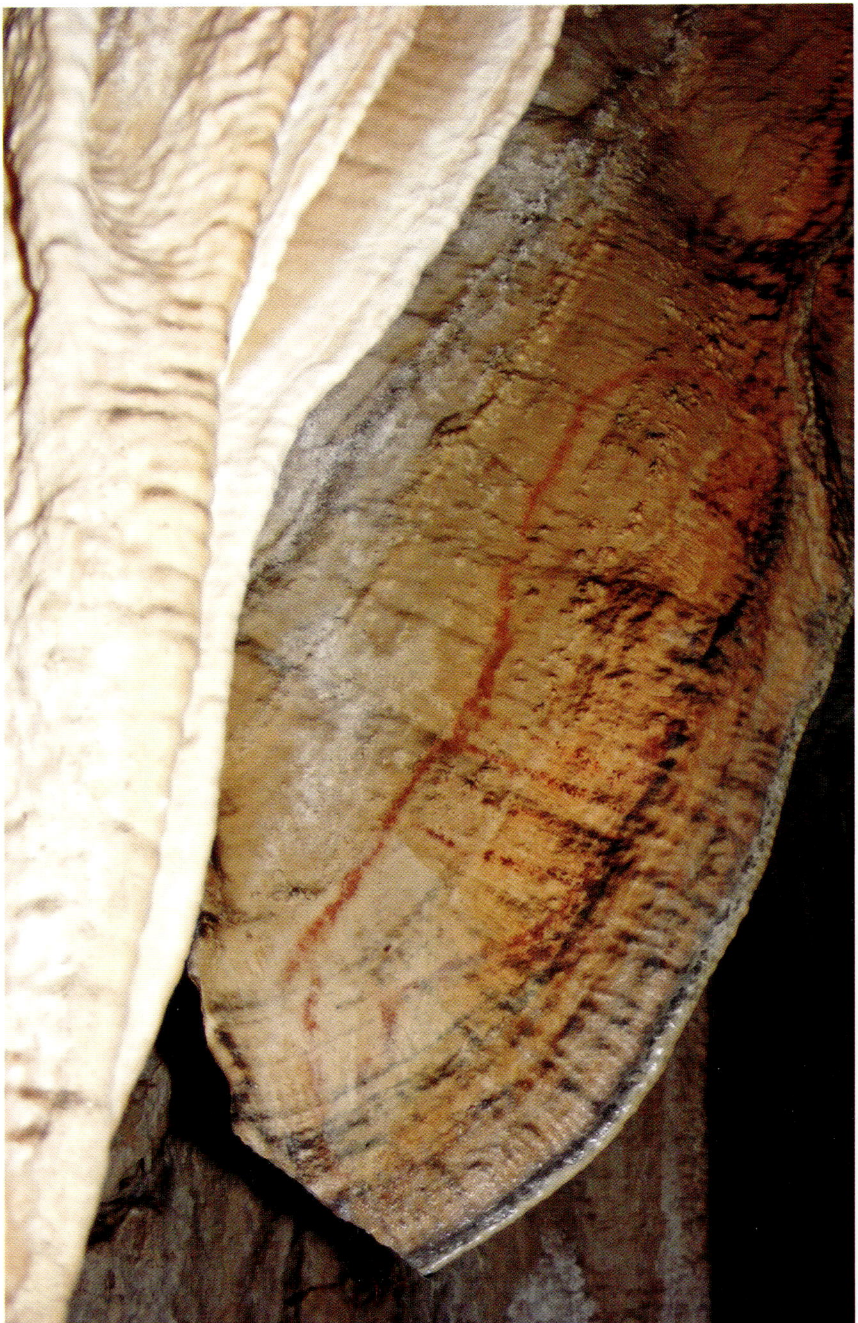

Solutrean horse on a drapery

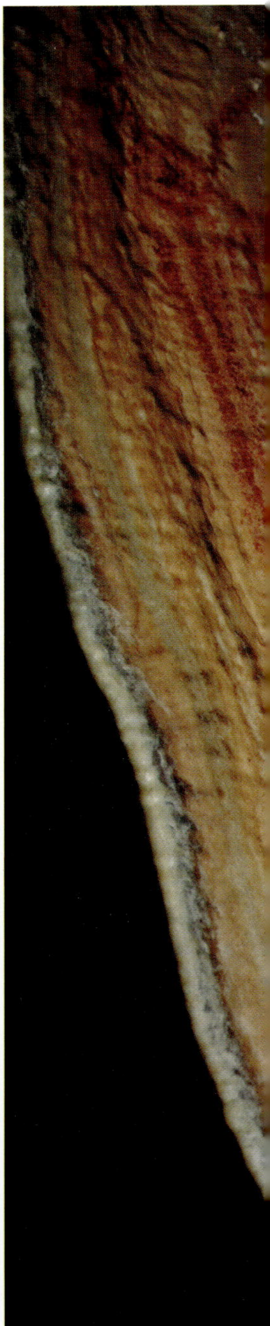

at levels corresponding to this period have also uncovered several loose stones with engravings and traces of pigment.

Another interesting technique, also datable by indirect methods to the Upper Palaeolithic (Gravettian), was used to create a panel on a large shelf in the Hall of the Cataclysm. On a surface covered with delicate speleothems, prehistoric artists applied liquid red pigment by blowing it with their mouths, creating several broad slanted bands whose significance still eludes us today.

The group of Magdalenian artistic expressions is dated to approximately 15,000 BP. In this period, human groups ventured into the Upper Galleries and marked restricted spaces with free designs and intersecting lines drawn in chalk or charcoal pencil. A considerable number of figurative motifs, which have not yet been precisely dated, are located in a small chamber in the Upper Galleries, where several columns were decorated with fusiform shapes in

There is a clear distinction between artistic expressions from the Pleistocene and those made by prehistoric societies of the Holocene —in other words, Neolithic and Chalcolithic or Copper Age humans.

red ink. Originally, they were believed to be fish—hence the name, Niche of Fish Forms—but today they are interpreted as seals. While excavating the Magdalenian levels, archaeologists came across a small stone with several engravings, most notably the figure of a duck. This invaluable piece of portable art is now on display in the Nerja Museum.

The art of productive societies, primarily created between the late Neolithic and early Chalcolithic, reflects the symbolism derived from consistent use of the cave for funerary purposes. In the Hall of the Sinkhole (closed to visitors due to ongoing archaeological investigations), there is a

Solutrean doe on the same drapery

panel with two schematic human figures drawn in red lines. They are popularly referred to as "The Dancers" based on their positions, although they could also be depictions of archers. These are the only artistic motifs in the entire cave system that were made in a chamber partially illuminated by natural light.

Several engravings in the Hall of the Kitchen, located in the Upper Galleries, and the Hall of the Cataclysm in the Show Galleries also date from the Neolithic-Chalcolithic transition period. Known as "bi-triangular forms", they conform to a known type of schematic anthropomorphic idol which usually appears on portable objects found at levels from this era. One of them has very pronounced female sexual attributes. Other familiar forms, also found on the slabs of several dolmen tombs, are "cupules", erosive depressions in the rock made by percussion with a harder hammer-stone. Clear examples, almost certainly associated with the megalithic funerary world, can be seen in the halls of the Nativity and Elephant Tusk. Virtually all these artistic creations were made at a time when the lower sector of the cave was given over to intense funerary use. In fact, the engravings in the Hall of the Cataclysm are associated with a shelf bearing the remains of two or three child skeletons, which were defleshed and completely coated in liquid red pigment.

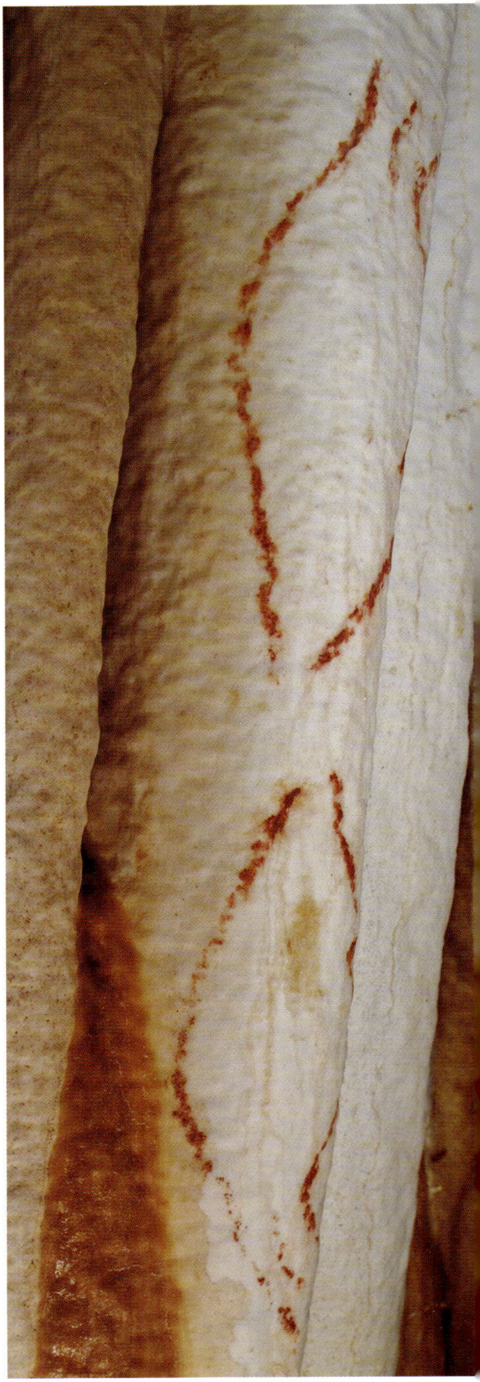

Figures in the Niche of Fish Forms

Solutrean horse head, Hall of the Cataclysm

Digital tracing of a complex panel, with the complete figures of a stag and a doe, two horse heads and one headless doe

Solutrean graphic code (series of dots and lines) arranged around the figure of a goat, "The Organ" formation

Solutrean graphic code (series of parallel lines), "The Organ"

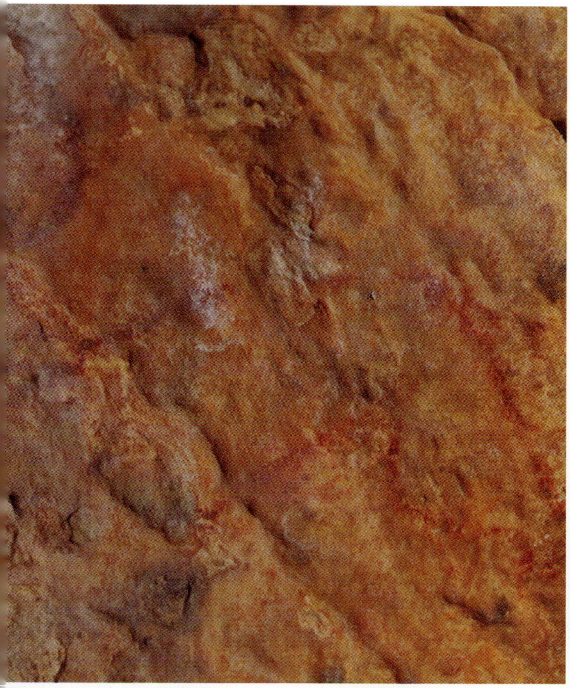

Magdalenian black lines painted on a shield

Solutrean doe drawn on "The Organ"

Chalcolithic engravings of schematic human figures

Solutrean stag, Niche of the Stag

Useful Information

Panoramic view of the Hall of the Waterfall

HELP US TO PRESERVE NERJA CAVE

Preserving the invaluable cultural and natural heritage of a cave visited by over 400,000 people each year is a difficult task that requires considerable resources and human effort. The presence of people inside the cave has an environmental impact that must be avoided or mitigated as much as possible. Fundación Pública de Servicios Cueva de Nerja (Nerja Cave Public Services Foundation) has decided to adopt a management strategy based on promoting and publishing the results of scientific research, one that strikes a healthy balance between providing public access to the cave and guaranteeing its conservation. Since 1959, the very year of the cave's discovery, research projects have been conducted here in different scientific fields, placing Nerja Cave at the vanguard of investigation into the subterranean environment. Today, the Instituto de Investigación (Research Institute) is responsible for designing and implementing conservation protocols based on that research.

The conduct of visitors to the cave is a crucial factor in its preservation. Compliance with the established visiting and conservation rules ensures that human impact on the cave is minimised. Some of the most important rules are explained below:

Touching the cave walls or speleothems can soil them, wear them down, interrupt their growth or even cause them to break. Therefore, visitors are not permitted to touch or alter geological formations in any way. Camera tripods and selfie sticks are not allowed as their use may accidentally damage the formations.

The cave is home to endemic and extremely sensitive fauna; we therefore ask that visitors respect any animals they may encounter during the tour and refrain from raising their voices.

Food remnants do not decompose easily inside the cave and can facilitate the growth of fungi that may damage the rock art. For this reason, food, juice and similar beverages are not allowed inside the cave.

The presence of coins, paper, plastic or any other foreign waste contaminates the cave. Therefore, please make sure not to leave anything behind in the cave; remember that it is a protected archaeological site of incalculable value.

Lighting must be kept low inside the cave to prevent the spread of "green sickness" on walls and speleothems. Any other light sources, such as camera flashes or electric torches, may blind other visitors and cause accidents, and their use is therefore prohibited.

Human presence alters the composition of the air inside the cave. It takes time for atmospheric levels to return to normal after visiting hours, which explains why the cave must close early each day.

Prehistoric rock art is extremely fragile. The presence of humans in the vicinity or direct lighting cause environmental changes that may damage the art in various ways. For this reason, the cave's rock art is not included in the tour itinerary.

LEARN MORE

A vital resource for learning more about Nerja Cave is the Nerja Museum, located in the heart of this lovely coastal town. This museum houses and safeguards the extraordinary collection of archaeological artefacts found in Nerja Cave and its environs, as well as the historical archive of the cavern.

There are also many printed and digital sources on Nerja Cave that provide further information about this remarkable site. Some of the best are the book series *Trabajos sobre la Cueva de Nerja* (Works on Nerja Cave), the micro-documentary series *Tres minutos con la Cueva de Nerja* (Three Min-

utes with Nerja Cave), available on YouTube and Facebook, and the videos and projects published on the Instituto de Investigación website, many of which are downloadable.

With this guide, Fundación Pública de Servicios Cueva de Nerja, committed to the research, conservation and dissemination of our heritage, aims to raise public awareness about the importance of the treasures held in Nerja Cave, encouraging visitors to have a respectful attitude and help us to preserve this natural and cultural heritage. We hope we have succeeded.

Thank you for visiting, and we look forward to seeing you soon!

Prehistory Gallery, Nerja Museum

Trabajos sobre la Cueva de Nerja series

- F. JORDÁ PARDO (ed.). VV.AA. *La Prehistoria de la Cueva de Nerja (Málaga).* 1986. Trabajos sobre la Cueva de Nerja, no. 1. Patronato de la Cueva de Nerja.

- F. MARÍN GIRÓN (ed.). VV.AA. *Investigación biológica y edafológica Cueva de Nerja (Málaga).* 1991. Trabajos sobre la Cueva de Nerja, no. 2. Patronato de la Cueva de Nerja.

- F. CARRASCO CANTOS (ed.). VV.AA. *Geología de la Cueva de Nerja.* 1993. Trabajos sobre la Cueva de Nerja, no. 3. Patronato de la Cueva de Nerja.

- J.L. SANCHIDRIÁN TORTI. *Arte rupestre de la Cueva de Nerja.* 1994. Trabajos sobre la Cueva de Nerja, no. 4. Patronato de la Cueva de Nerja.

- M. PELLICER CATALÁN and A. MORALES MUÑIZ (eds.). VV.AA. *Fauna de la Cueva de Nerja I. Salas de la Mina y de la Torca, campañas 1980-82.* 1995. Trabajos sobre la Cueva de Nerja, no. 5. Patronato de la Cueva de Nerja.

- M. PELLICER CATALÁN and P. ACOSTA MARTÍNEZ (eds.). VV.AA. *El Neolítico y Calcolítico de la Cueva de Nerja en el contexto andaluz.* 1997. Trabajos sobre la Cueva de Nerja, no. 6. Patronato de la Cueva de Nerja.

- Y. DEL ROSAL PADIAL (ed.). VV.AA. *Análisis, impacto y evolución de los biofilms fotosintéticos en espeleotemas. El caso de la Cueva de Nerja (Málaga, España).* 2017. Trabajos sobre la Cueva de Nerja, no. 7. Fundación Pública de Servicios Cueva de Nerja.

Tres minutos con la Cueva de Nerja series (in Spanish)

0. **Introduction to the documentary series.** Luis-Efrén Fernández Rodríguez

1. **Calcite for Two: Calcite Rafts and Cave Cones.** Cristina Liñán Baena

2. **Lights of the Past.** María de los Ángeles Medina Alcaide

3. **Drawing in the Dark.** José María Cobos Pastor

4. **Tiny and Exclusive: Cave Fauna.** Yolanda del Rosal Padial

5. **Pages of the Distant Past.** Rosa María Ruiz Márquez

6. **Geology and Archaeology, a Natural Pair.** Eneko Iriarte Avilés

Other informative videos (in Spanish)

- **Plaquette with Engraving.** Rosa María Ruiz Márquez

- **The Colour of Life, the Colour of Death.** Luis-Efrén Fernández Rodríguez

- **The Historical Archive of Fundación Cueva de Nerja.** Antonio Montesino Baca and Juan Bautista Salado Escaño

- **Pepita: An Epipalaeolithic Skeleton at the Nerja Museum.** Juan Bautista Salado Escaño, Elena Pérez González, Rafael Ruiz de la Linde and Francisco Torres Ruiz

GLOSSARY

Biogeography: the branch of biology that studies the geographical distribution of animals and plants.

BP: abbreviation of "before present", a time scale widely used in various scientific fields. For the purposes of archaeological dating, the "present" is defined as the year 1950.

Chalcolithic: a prehistoric period, also called the Copper Age, that began between the sixth and fifth millennia BP. The majority of known funerary activities in the cave correspond to Chalcolithic societies.

Ecosystem: a community of living organisms that share a specific space where they interact with each other and their environment.

Endemic: said of a species or taxon unique to a defined geographical area. Endemic species are more vulnerable to human activity and other environmental factors which may pose a threat to their survival.

Epipalaeolithic: the intervening period between the Palaeolithic and the rise of the first Neolithic productive societies. It is considered to have begun at the end of the last glaciation, roughly 12,000 BP. This period is characterised by the appearance of small lithic tools adapted to new needs.

Evolution: the gradual transformation of species through changes over successive generations.

Figurative motif: in prehistoric rock or portable art, depictions of animals or human figures are called "figurative" motifs to distinguish them from symbols and other graphic expressions whose significance is less clear.

Gravettian: an industry named after the French site of La Gravette, spanning the period from approximately 25,000 to 21,000 BP. This is the oldest major lithic culture documented in the cave's archaeological record.

Holocene: the current epoch of the Quaternary period that began 10,000 years ago.

Magdalenian: the last industry of the Upper Palaeolithic, named after the French rock shelter of La Madeleine and dated to between 15,000 and 12,000 BP.

Miocene: a geological epoch extending from 23 to 5.3 million years ago.

Mousterian: a Middle Palaeolithic culture associated with Neanderthal populations. In Nerja, some findings have been dated to the final stages of this period (around 45,000 BP), and several examples of Mousterian stone tools have appeared at the bottom of excavations in the Entrance Hall.

Neolithic: a period between 7,500 and 4,500 BP, when the coastal regions of the Iberian Peninsula began to adopt lifestyles typical of a productive economy (agriculture and animal husbandry) and pottery was introduced.

Palaeolithic: in general terms, this is the longest period of human history, characterised by gradual anatomical modifications in our genus that made us what we are today, modern humans. Palaeolithic societies had environmental foraging economies based on hunting, fishing and gathering.

Phototroph: an organism that transforms energy from light into chemical energy.

Pleistocene: first epoch of the Quaternary period which lasted from 2.6 million to 10,000 years ago. It is divided into different stages, such as the Middle Pleistocene (0.78–0.13 million years ago) and Upper Pleistocene (0.13–0.01 million years ago).

Pliocene: a geological epoch extending from 5.3 to 2.6 million years ago.

Quaternary: a period extending from 2.6 million years ago to the present. It is divided into two epochs, the Pleistocene and the Holocene.

Rock art: prehistoric paintings or engravings on the walls and ceilings of caves and rock shelters. When found on portable objects for everyday or religious use, it is called "portable art".

Solutrean: lithic culture of the Upper Palaeolithic, between 22,000 and 16,000 BP. This industry is characterised by beautiful stone tools fashioned using flat retouch or thinning techniques. Solutrean populations are responsible for a large part of the rock paintings in the "prehistoric sanctuary" of Nerja Cave.

WE WOULD LIKE TO ACKNOWLEDGE THE COLLABORATION OF ALL THE ORGANISATIONS AND INDIVIDUALS WHO MADE THIS PUBLICATION POSSIBLE.
FUNDACIÓN PS CUEVA DE NERJA
INSTITUTO DE INVESTIGACIÓN CUEVA DE NERJA

PUBLISHER
Editorial Palacios y Museos
EDITORIAL COORDINATION
Editorial Palacios y Museos / Anabel Hernández
TEXT
Cristina Liñán Baena, Yolanda del Rosal Padial and Luis-Efrén Fernández Rodríguez. Instituto de Investigación Cueva de Nerja and Fundación Pública de Servicios Cueva de Nerja
TRANSLATION
Polisemia, S.L.

IMAGES
All photographs in this guide were taken by Mariano Ibáñez Heredia, except the following: pp. 27 and 57, Archivo Fundación PS Cueva de Nerja; pp. 46b, 49b–49e, 64–67 and 71a, IICN; pp. 35, 41b and 42–43, Agapito Sanchidrián Torti; pp. 33, 38–39, Víctor Ferrer Rico; p. 69b, Antonio Torres Riesco; pp. 76–77, Foto Guerrero; p. 31, E. Diaz.
COLLABORATION
Fundación PS Cueva de Nerja and Instituto de Investigación Cueva de Nerja
DESIGN AND LAYOUT
Nicolás García Marque
PRINTERS
Villena Artes Gráficas
PLANS
IICN
GRAPHIC RECREATION
Enrique Díaz

ISBN: 978-84-8003-738-9 (1st ED., 2nd PRINTING)
LEGAL DEPOSIT: M-2438-2019

PRINTED IN SPAIN.

P&M EDICIONES
Museo de Nerja
FUNDACIÓN Cueva de Nerja
IICN